The Secret

The Secret
ISBN: 979-8-9851553-4-1
Written by Baxter Kruger

First published 1994, republished 2023

About the Author

Baxter has been married to Beth for 40 years. They have four children and four grandchildren and live in Brandon, Mississippi. He received his Ph.D. at Kings College, Aberdeen University in Scotland under Professor James. B. Torrance. Dr. Kruger is the author of 9 books, including the international bestsellers, *The Shack Revisited, Patmos*, and his early small book, *The Parable of the Dancing God*, numerous essays, and hundreds of hours of teaching, and a variety of online studies—all available at perichoresis.org. Dr. Kruger has traveled the world for 30 years proclaiming the good news of our inclusion in Jesus and his relationship with his Father in the Spirit. He enjoys cooking crawfish, hand carving fishing lures, playing golf, and loves spending time with his grandchildren.

Cover Design: Tom Carroll, South Australia
Illustrations: Dianne C. Bryan Jackson, MS
Book layout: Karen Thompson, Western Australia

Other Titles Available From C. Baxter Kruger:

Patmos

The Shack Revisited

Across All Worlds

Jesus and the Undoing of Adam

The Great Dance

God Is For Us

HOME

The Parable of the Dancing God

A Note on the Word *Perichoresis*

Genuine acceptance removes fear and hiding, and creates freedom to know and be known. In this freedom arises a fellowship and sharing so honest and open and real that the persons involved dwell in one another. There is union without loss of individual identity. When one weeps, the other tastes salt. It is only in the Triune relationship of Father, Son and Spirit that personal relationship of this order exists, and the early Church used the word "perichoresis" to describe it. The good news is that Jesus Christ has drawn us within this relationship and its fullness and life are to be played out in each of us and in all creation.

For more information on Dr. C. Baxter Kruger or Perichoresis go to Perichorises.org

Imagine an eight-year-old kid at the fair. There he is, in the midst of everything a kid dreams about. Exciting rides, caramel apples and cotton candy, games and prizes - all are within his reach. And he is taking full advantage of the moment. But suddenly he realizes that he has been separated from his parents. He is *lost.* Sheer terror seizes his little soul. In a split second he moves from having the time of his life to being so panic-stricken that he no longer even knows there is a fair. His freedom to see and enjoy the good and wonderful things that are all around him has vanished into thin air.

What this story is telling us is that what happens to our insides shapes the way we experience what is outside of us. Our insides can be so shredded we lose sight of the great and awesome things that are all around us. We no longer see them as great and awesome. And when that happens, we lose our freedom to enjoy them.

I think the kid at the fair is a parable of human life, it is a picture of what is happening to us, of why our joy and contentment are so fleeting, of why life can be so painful and meaningless. Again and again we encounter something that overwhelms our insides. It may well be that we do not even know it. The internal shredding, so to speak, may not even reach the level of our conscious feelings, much less the intensity of feelings that we see in the kid at the fair. But the shredding is happening, and the effect is the same. The bewilderment inside short-circuits our capacity to behold the glory of life around us and thus shuts down our freedom to live in it. And we don't live in it. Our living becomes as empty as the laughter of the lady who did not get the punch line of the joke.

It is not that the glory goes away. It is just that we can no longer see it. We look right into the smile of a little girl and see nothing. There she stands, a sheer miracle, the living embodiment of beauty, and she is smiling at *us*, eager to share life. But we look right through her, smile and all. We do the same with other people, with flowers, with music, with work, and baseball. Their wonder and glory just don't register with us. They appear pale to us, mundane, even boring and meaningless. I don't think that we are consciously aware of what is happening. Rarely do we tell ourselves that this person or that flower is boring. We just don't see them for what they are, and as a result, their presence does not touch us or mean anything to us. Before we know it we have flown through a week - maybe even months and years - with our eyes glazed over. We may be alive, but we have missed out on living life. For we cannot relate to, much less enjoy, what we cannot see.

Dwarfdom

Let me relate a story to you that illustrates what this kind of blindness does to us. It comes from C. S. Lewis' splendid tale, *The Chronicles of Narnia.*[1] The scene is of a beautiful land on a clear day. The whole earth is full of glory, alive with a radiance that only our best, most glorious days can hint at. It is Narnia, the promised and

1 C. S. Lewis, *The Chronicles of Narnia*, vol. 7: *The Last Battle* (New York: Collier Books, Macmillan Publishing Company, 1956). See also Lewis' superb books, *Till We Have Faces* (New York: Harcourt Brace Jovanovich, 1957) and *The Great Divorce* (New York: Collier Books, Macmillan Publishing Company, 1946)

longed-for land. Several of the heroes of the story are walking around with increasing awe and irrepressible joy, never having even imagined anything so beautiful, so intensely alive, so real, so good.

But also present is a bitter little band of scowling Dwarfs. They are not exploring. There is no light of wonder in their eyes. They have no joy. They are, in fact, huddled in a tight circle on the ground. Far from knowing themselves to be in a beautiful land on a clear day, they believe they are trapped in a "pitch-black, poky, smelly little hole of a stable."[2]

Lucy, one of the heroes of the story, shouts to the Dwarfs: "But it isn't dark, you poor stupid Dwarfs. Can't you see? Look up! Look round! Can't you see the sky and the trees and the flowers? Can't you see *me*?"[3]

One of the scowling Dwarfs, named Diggle, blurts out in exasperation: "How in the name of all Humbug can I see what ain't there? And how can I see you any more than you can see me in this pitch darkness?"[4]

Instantly a bolt of grief shoots through Lucy's heart. Then an idea comes to her. She snatches up some wild violets and shoves them toward Diggle. "Listen, Dwarf," she says, "even if your eyes are wrong, perhaps your nose is all right: can you smell that?"[5] Smell he can, but far from smelling fresh violets, Diggle smells

2 Lewis, *The Last Battle*, p. 144.
3 Lewis, *The Last Battle*, p. 144.
4 Lewis, *The Last Battle*, p. 144.
5 Lewis, *The Last Battle*, p. 145.

stable-litter, and is so deeply offended he takes a swipe at her.

At this point, the great lion Aslan appears. Aslan is the supreme hero of the story and the one responsible for the existence and the glory of Narnia. Lucy, in her bewildered grief over the blind Dwarfs, immediately implores Aslan to do something to help them. What follows is fascinating:

> Aslan raised his head and shook his mane. Instantly a glorious feast appeared on the Dwarfs' knees: pies and tongues and pigeons and trifles and ices, and each Dwarf had a goblet of good wine in his right hand. But it wasn't much use. They began eating and drinking greedily enough, but it was clear that they couldn't taste it properly. They thought they were eating and drinking only the sort of things you might find in a Stable. One said he was trying to eat hay and another said he had got a bit of an old turnip and a third said he'd found a raw cabbage leaf. And they raised golden goblets of rich red wine to their lips and said "Ugh! Fancy drinking dirty water out of a trough that a donkey's been at! Never thought we'd come to this".[6]

This is a truly tragic situation. The Dwarfs sit in the open on a splendid cloudless day. Before them is a luscious feast called forth by the King (admittedly you would have to be British to think of

6 Lewis, *The Last Battle*, p. 145

this as a feast, but use your imagination). They have the golden goblets in their hands. But, as Lucy said, their eyes are all wrong, and so is everything else, dreadfully so. They actually drink the rich red wine of the promised land and taste only dirty water from a donkey's trough!

Note carefully that the problem is not that the Dwarfs have been excluded from the glory of Narnia. They are every bit as much in Narnia as are the heroes. In fact, it would be impossible for the Dwarfs to be any closer to Narnia than they already are. But their eyes are wrong.[7] And the absence of proper seeing leaves them incapable of experiencing Narnia as *Narnia*. Like the kid at the fair, the Dwarfs' blindness robs them of the joy of Narnia and thus leaves them scowling and bitter.

This is what happens to us. It is not that we are excluded from Narnia, so to speak. The feast is ours. We daily dine on the bounty of the King's royal food and raise his golden goblets of rich red wine. But something rather like an optical illusion keeps happening and we do not see properly. We do not see who we really are, where we are, and with what glory we are involved. And this optical illusion, this absence of light, this absence of proper seeing, destroys our ability to experience the feast as a *feast*, the fair as a *fair*, life as *life*. Without seeing the glory we have no freedom to live in it. And life inevitably becomes a joyless, boring, meaningless routine-sometimes, even dreadful.

---

7 See Matthew 6:22-23

The Troll's Trick

But why are we so blind? What creates the optical illusion? What is it that keeps us from seeing properly? We already have the first part of the answer in the story of the kid at the fair. He could not see properly because his insides were shredded. It is the same with us. Our hearts get shredded, and instantly we lose our security, our hope, our assurance. When that happens we become so anxious and fearful and panic-stricken we lose our capacity to notice.

But why do we lose our security and hope and assurance? What causes our insides to be shredded? The problem is that there is something like a nasty old troll lurking in the shadows of our lives.[8] He keeps himself hidden, while his beady little eyes are riveted on our hearts. He knows how human beings function. He knows the sequence: Security produces freedom to see and seeing brings joy. So he is watching carefully, watching for the first inkling of security or hope or assurance. When he sees it, he sets the wheels into motion, the wheels of a diabolical scheme tailor-made to suffocate our security. The mechanism is already in place and well-greased. It takes a mere whisper at the opportune moment to start it moving. And we are so ignorant of his schemes, we do not even realize what is happening.

With far greater clarity than human beings, the troll understands that the only security in the universe comes from knowing that God the Father Almighty has embraced us in Jesus Christ. So his

8 See II Corinthians 4:3-4 and II Timothy 2:26

schemes are designed to keep us either from knowing the truth of the Father's embrace or from believing it. Either way the only basis of real security is eclipsed, and that means that blindness and thus empty living are only a moment away.

The troll is a master shame specialist. He excels at exploiting our guilt and our wounds. It is as though he carries a shovel around with him and digs up all the black stuff that we try to keep buried. He digs up our failures, especially the ones that we are most ashamed of-whether we did them or they were done to us, it doesn't matter to him—and he drags them out so that we have to feel them and know them all over again. And then he whispers from the shadows that we are worthless, no good, no count, sorry, nothing. His favorite phrase is "*I am not...*" and he whispers it to us so subtly we think we are saying it: "I am not acceptable. I am not adequate. I am not smart enough, not good enough, not capable, not creative, not special. I am not doing it right. I am not going to make it."

But this is only the beginning. He also whispers lies about God. He tells us that God is like our father who beat us or abused us or rejected us. He tells us that God is like a boring old professor who sits in his ivory tower mumbling profundities to himself. He tells us that God is like a bookkeeper who watches us, pencil in hand, from a distance, only to keep tabs on how well we are stacking up against His rules. He tells us that God is just a divine version of the nerds that pass for preachers on TV, or that He is unapproachable in His self-importance like so many of the religious people we know. He tells us that God is like "the force" in *Star Wars*—incomprehensible, unknowable, unnameable and useless to the average person.

You see what the troll is doing. He is setting us up. He so shames us with our failures, it is almost impossible for us to believe that we belong to God. His lies that God is like our father or the bookkeeper have already got us believing that God does not like us. So his whisper "I am not… " easily leads to "therefore God could not possibly want me," "therefore God is not interested in me in the least," "therefore God has abandoned all hope for me, given up on me and walked away." And if that doesn't work, well, what security can possibly come from knowing that you belong to some unknowable force, or a divine nerd, or a boring old professor?

Over the years the evil one has woven his lies and accusations into our thinking. Together they have produced a deep-seated suspicion within us: "I am alone, lost, abandoned, rejected." He has carefully nudged the suspicion to within a hair's breadth of being a conclusion, a belief. We are primed and don't even know it. He merely waits and watches in the shadows, not only for the first sign of security, but even more important, for something negative to happen in our experience. Then he whispers his final word to us: "See, I told you so." And in that moment the suspicion becomes a conclusion. We believe we are alone, lost, abandoned, rejected.

What does believing this lie do to us? It absolutely shreds our insides. Whether we realize it or not, our security and hope and assurance are overwhelmed, and we immediately lose our freedom to see. In a split second, our capacity to notice, to behold, to discover, is short-circuited. And we don't notice, and not noticing means that life gives us no joy. It leaves us empty. And none of us can live with emptiness, so we desperately plunge ourselves into hot pursuit of something we believe will fill us, or we run from the pain. In all likelihood we never even know what we are doing.

The Truth

But the troll is a liar, the father of lies[9] For the truth is, you are not lost. You have been found by God the Father Almighty in His Son Jesus Christ. That is who you are. You are not abandoned, alone or rejected. You have been claimed, accepted and embraced by the Father in His Son.[10] The verdict of God spoken to you in Jesus is not "I am not," but "*Thou art Mine!*"

9 See John 8:44.
10 See II Corinthians 5:14-21; Ephesians 1:3-13; Colossians 1:19ff

Jesus Christ has taken your failures and wrongness, your guilt and shame, your alienation—the very things the troll digs up—and destroyed them all on the cross.[11] All the blackness has been forgiven, wiped out, put to death. It is done, finished, gone forever. He has put an end to everything that alienates us from his Father and life in His house. For that is why he came. He was sent to prepare a place for us in the Father's house,[12] a place in the circle of the Father's acceptance, love and delight. And he has prepared a place for you, made room for you in the Father's life.

But you do not know it. The troll has you believing that you are the kid abandoned and lost at the fair. You do not know that you have been found—welcomed and embraced by the Father Himself. You do not know that Jesus Christ is your shepherd,[13] sent by the Father, or that he has searched you out, found you, bathed you and completely cleansed you, laid you on his shoulders and carried you home to his Father. You think that God is a bookkeeper or an unknowable force somewhere out there. You know nothing of the Father's acceptance and forgiveness, of His great passion for you, and of the supreme delight He has in you.

You are a sitting duck. Defenseless. Without a real knowledge of the fact that God the Father Almighty has laid hold of you with an eternal grip in Jesus Christ, you have no answer when the evil

11 See Colossians 2:13-14
12 See John 14:1-3.
13 See John 10:11-16.

one whispers. Whatever hope you have managed to find is blown away like a dandelion in the breeze. Your insides are shredded. Your security is gone. You see no glory. Your life is joyless.

It is time for you to wake up and see the light! It is time for you to know the truth.[14] It is time for you to know who God actually is, and who you are, and to know what great and awesome thing God your Father has actually made of you in His Son by the power of the Spirit.

"Immanuel."[15] That is God's one word summary of it all. You know what "Immanuel" means, don't you? It means "God is with us." Note carefully that it does not mean God was with us or that God will be with us. It means God is with us and we are with God. This is not a neat religious idea. And it is certainly not an invitation that depends upon our religious performance. Immanuel is a rock-solid fact established by God. It is a divine declaration of the way things really are. God has not abandoned us. He has embraced us and made us His in Jesus Christ.

The Light of Life

But what exactly does it mean to say that God is with us and we are with God in Jesus Christ? It certainly means that in His great passion for us God has stepped forward and established a relationship with us. He has claimed us as His own, blotted out our

14 See John 8:31-32.
15 See Matthew 1:23.

failures, removed everything that alienates us from Him, redeemed us, accepted us and welcomed us into His family. So at the very least, Immanuel means that we are not separated from God. We are not absent from Him and He is not absent from us. We are together and God is thrilled about it.

But there is something else, something marvelous, indeed astonishing, that is being said here about us, about you and me and our humanity, about our human existence. In this one word, "Immanuel," God is telling us that He has no intention of being God without us! He is telling us that the reason He made us is to share His life with us. For sharing life is the purpose of being with someone. But even here we are only scratching the surface. For Immanuel is not only a statement about God's intention. It is a statement about what is happening in our lives now. Immanuel means that God is now sharing His life with us and we are now sharing in God's life. We are inside the circle of God's life now, and thus the life we are living is not our own. Our life is nothing less than a participation in God's life!

Let me share a story that brings this home to us. Several years ago, while I was sorting through mail, my son and one of his buddies strolled into the den where I was sitting. I did not know his friend at all. We were complete strangers. I didn't even know his name. But what happened has become to me a concrete picture of Immanuel.

While this little boy did not know me or what I was like, my son did. My son had a relationship with me. He knew my love for him and my delight in him. He knew the assurance of my acceptance. He was at-home with me and thus free to be himself, free to come into my presence and play. And he did just that. In the freedom of acceptance he sauntered into my presence, bounded onto the couch and engaged me in play. The next thing I knew, we were rolling around on the floor, wrestling and laughing and having the time of our lives. And his buddy was right in there with us.

Later on I realized that something quite critical had taken place, a parable had been enacted. Think of it this way. Suppose that you deleted my son from the equation for a moment. Suppose that his buddy walked into the den alone. I suspect, given that we were complete strangers, that he would never have bounded onto the couch and engaged me in play. Without my son's presence there would have been no assurance of acceptance, no at-homeness, and thus no freedom to saunter into my presence.

But my son *was* present. And the marvelous thing that happened was that my son's relationship with me, his knowledge of my acceptance, his freedom to come into my presence, worked its way into his buddy's heart. It was simple, yet remarkable. This boy was ushered into something that was not his and he got to share in it. He got to share in my son's relationship with me. He participated in my son's freedom. He played in it.

Now, here is the question. Could it be that something very much like this is going on in your life but you do not know it? Could it be

that you, like my son's buddy, have been included in someone else's life? Could it be that your interests and burdens, your delights and loves, are not, strictly speaking, yours at all? What if they have their origin in someone else who is secretly sharing them with you? What if your creativity and work, your love for your family, your delight in music, golf and fishing, your concern for things to be right, your joy in giving, all originate not with you but with someone else far greater than you, someone who loves you so much that He shares His excellence, His beauty, His wholeness and fullness with you?

That is exactly, I believe, what Immanuel means. We have all been given a staggering gift, the gift of participating in Jesus Christ's relationship with God the Father Almighty in the fellowship of the Spirit. This is the secret of your existence. You are a participant in Jesus' life. Just like my son's buddy, you have been ushered into something that is not yours, included in it, and you are living in it.[16] The troll may well have you believing his whisper "I am not... ," but the truth is you are living nothing less than Jesus' life with his Father.

God is not a bookkeeper or an old professor or some kind of

16 See Colossians 1:27

divine black hole who is so angst-ridden, so lonely and bored and needy he sucks the life out of everything around him. God exists as a triune relationship—Father, Son and Spirit. And it is not a dead or empty relationship. The Father, Son and Spirit are not like three bronze statues in the park—speechless, motionless, heartless. The Father likes His Son. He loves him, is absolutely thrilled with him, bursting with pride over him.[17] And the Son adores his Father, loves Him with all of his heart, soul, mind and strength in the freedom and fellowship of the Spirit. Far from being frozen in some lifeless pose, the Father, Son and Spirit live in a circle of eager and lavish hospitality. It is a circle of passionate embracing, of mutual acceptance, delight and love, which issues forth not in sadness or depression or misery but in unchained life—joyous, overflowing fellowship. The early theologians of the church were quite right when they spoke of the triune life of God as a divine dance. It is not dead, but alive, good, right, unstifled, overflowing, creative.

You probably know the Bible story about Jesus turning water into wine.[18] What has always struck me as odd about the story is the fact that Jesus asked the servants to get the water for him. Think about it. If Jesus can turn water into wine, he surely does not need anyone to get water for him, does he? Of course not. So why does he ask the servants for help? Because that is the kind of person he is. He delights in including others in what he is doing.

I think this story is a picture of the very reason Jesus Christ

17 See Matthew 3:17; 17:5 and John 5:19-20.

18 See John 2:1ff.

became a human being. Have you ever thought about that? Why would the Son trouble himself with becoming a human being? Why would he do such a thing? It is a lot like grandparents when they get down on all fours to play with their new grandchild. The whole point is to share life with their loved ones. Innately, they know that to communicate they must stoop to the infant's level and do their dead level best to enter into the grandchild's world. Of course, what we call "the incarnation" is far more profound than this, but the basic idea is the same. The Son of God became human so that he could share his life with us in a way that could actually touch us.

But the troll has lied to us for so long about God, we think He is way off up there in Heaven. All the troll's lies about God are designed to keep us from knowing about Jesus' presence, about Immanuel. And it seems to me that the troll has done a fairly good job, even—and perhaps especially—in the Church. For what is basic about our perception of God and ourselves is that we are separated. We see God on one side of the table and ourselves on the other. God puts His rules and commands on the table and we are supposed to respond and keep the rules. Religion is the whole bundle of things that we come up with to put on the table to answer God for ourselves.

But this is all wrongheaded. Besides the fact that God is interested in far more than our keeping rules, this way of thinking leaves Jesus out of the picture. There is no Immanuel in the equation. It is not Christian at all, for the simple truth is that now God is on both sides of the table. The Son of God became human.[19] So now you have the Father on one side and the Son on the other—in our place, sitting in our chair. And they are sharing life together in the fellowship of the Spirit.[20]

Why? Why did the Son come across to our side of the table? The answer is simple. He did this so he could then share his life with us. He was born to be the mediator.[21] He came so that he could share with us the life and wholeness that he has in his relationship with his Father from all eternity.[22] That is a breathtaking thought when we stop long enough to take it in. But it is no mere thought: It is the plain truth.

The gospel is all about the fact that the Son of God, who enjoys life with his Father in the fellowship of the Spirit, became human—came across to our side of the table—so that he could share nothing less than this life with us. And he was sent not only to share this life with us but also to deal once and for all with our alienation from it. What good would it do for the grandparent to stoop to the grandchild if the grandchild were blind, deaf and mute? But, if in stooping, the grandparent could also heal, well then that is the point. Jesus came to share his rich life with us, and he came to do what was necessary—even at profound cost to himself—to heal us so that we could know and live in his life with him.

The fact that Jesus Christ has come means that you are not alone,

19 See John 1:1-3, 14.
20 See Matthew 3: 16-17 and 11:27
21 See I Timothy 2:5 and Hebrews 8:6; 9:15.
22 See Matthew 11:27-30.

and therefore that you are not worthless, inadequate, wrong, alien. The Father has made you blessed in His Son.[23] He has included you in everything that Jesus is to Him and in everything that they share together. You are clothed in surpassing dignity and glory and fullness right now,[24] and not just clothed—you are living in it. Just like my son's buddy, you are included in something that is not yours, and you are right in the middle of it. You are living in Jesus' excellence and fullness and glory, in his righteousness and beauty and passion, in his life with his Father. You are alive with the life of the Triune God.

23 See Ephesians 1:3
24 See Colossians 2:9-10.

What You Know But Never Knew

Let me tell you another story that will help clarify what I am saying. On a plane, recently, I sat by a biologist. Actually, he called himself a "systematic, evolutionary microbiologist"! He was returning from what seemed to me to be very like an Indiana Jones type expedition in the Caribbean. It was, in fact, a research trip dedicated to studying various species of plants.

Now, I admit, I am not a big plant man. Talking about plants, especially rare species that the average person does not even know exist, is not my idea of fun. But this guy was so excited I could not help but get caught up in his enthusiasm. Far from being dry and crusty, this man had fire in his belly and was absolutely thrilled with his work.

He launched into this story about plants that were on the verge of extinction, how important they were, what could be done to save them and why we must save them. He just could not bear the thought that we had already lost and were now losing whole species of plants to extinction. He even pulled out his napkin and drew diagrams and charts. I must say, I learned more botany in that stretch of time than I had learned in years of schooling.

When he finished, I leaned over and asked one simple question. "Where," I asked, "did you get your passion for plants?" It caught him off-guard and he looked at me like I had a third eye. I said, "I mean, it is not every day that you meet someone who has such a deep burden for the welfare of plants. I am just curious as to its origin. Did you grow up around botanists? Are your parents botanists? Did you just decide one day that you were going to love plants?" He said that he had never really thought about it much. And we both said, laughingly, "It probably just evolved!"

But then I pulled out my napkin and drew three interrelated circles, with the Father written in one circle and the Son and Spirit in the others. I pointed to the circle with the Son's name in it and said, "I know the origin of your deep passion for plants. There is only one human being in the universe who really cares for plants. He is delighted in his Father's creation, burdened for its welfare and preservation. He knows the plants by name, every one of them. And I know who you are. You are a participant in Jesus Christ's passion for his Father's creation.

"That fire in your belly is not yours. It does not have its origin in you. It comes from Jesus Christ. He puts his passion for his Father's plants in you. He humbly shares his delight in them, his burden for their welfare, his desire for their wholeness with you through his invisible Spirit. And you are living in it. You go to sleep at night, wake up in the morning, and work all day in his concerns and creative ideas. There is far more going on in your life than you ever imagined. You are living in Jesus' life, participating in the relationship that Jesus Christ has with his Father in the fellowship of the Spirit. You live in the circle of the Triune life of God and you are not sure that God even exists!"

Immanuel is not a theory. It is the secret. Jesus Christ is not tucked off in some closet in heaven waiting for a day to come when he can become a real factor in the universe. He is the Lord our God with us. He is the one in and by and through whom all things exist and are held together, including you. Wake up! "I am the light of the world, the one who follows me shall not live in the darkness, but shall have the secret of life."[25] Do you not see who you are and with whom you are involved? Do you not see what is happening in your life, what great and astounding thing has been conferred upon you?

Let me tell another story. A young mother walked into my office with a stack of newsletters in her hand. She plopped them down on my desk and exclaimed, "I feel like a pile of manure! I have been reading these newsletters from friends and missionaries and they are all out there doing these wonderful things for God. And it just hit me what a worthless life I have. For Pete's sake, I do three loads of laundry a day, and when I am not doing laundry I am grocery shopping, and when I am not grocery shopping I am unloading the groceries or cooking them or cleaning up after cooking them.

And somewhere in there I am trying to keep this mess of a house presentable, stay in touch with three kids, keep them clothed and on schedule and find a little time for my husband. I am too tired even to read my Bible. What do I have to offer God?

"Wait!" I said. "Just wait a minute. We need to punch the pause

25 John 8:12.

button and rethink all of this. I happen to know that just yesterday you spent two hours shopping for a coat for your daughter to keep her warm. And not just any coat, mind you, but one that she would like, that would be large enough to wear next year but not look like it, and one that was on sale! And I happen to know that you found the right one exactly. Now here is my question: Where did your concern for your daughter come from? I mean, did you just decide that you were going to be a good mother and flip a switch that created this burden for your daughter's welfare? What is the origin of your love for her or for your family, or your concern that they eat right every day, that they are nurtured? Where did you get this burden for a neat and orderly household?

"You are thinking like a Deist. You are thinking that God created this universe, wound it up like a great clock, set it running and then stepped out of the picture.

You are thinking that God is not here. And you are thinking that all that is going on in your life, your cooking and cleaning and grocery shopping, your love for your children and husband and your concern for their welfare and all that that generates, are all outside the circle of God's life. And because you are thinking this way you're very frustrated, you have lost the fullness and joy of it all, and you are desperately trying to figure out how to do all of this and then tack on something for God.

"You are missing the point. And the point is that Jesus Christ is not up there waiting for you to do something for him. He is here in you. He is sharing his burden for his sheep (your family) and their livelihood with you. And you wake up in it, live in it all day, and you really love it. It makes you sing. But you do not see it for what it actually is. It is not your burden and delight, but his, and there is no more holy thing in all the world than cooking a meal for your family. For that is nothing short of God the Father Himself, through His Son and in the Spirit, sharing His royal feast with His loved ones. It is a divine event!

"There is far more going on in your life than you ever dreamed. If you do not see it, you will die the slow and painful death of acedia—an ever intensifying boredom that is so deep and pervasive you lose all passion. You will raise golden goblets of rich red wine to your lips and never taste it. And you will despair in the frustration of never having a glass of good wine!"

Let me share one more story. I was having dinner recently with a professional golfer who is also a Christian. He leaned over to me and with great seriousness asked, "How does God fit into golf?" I know he was serious, earnestly so. I could see a profound dilemma in his eyes. For in his heart he wanted to play golf—the game

thrilled him—but in his head he could not quite figure how this was remotely related to honoring God, unless he managed to win on occasion and could then give the glory to God. He was torn.

His question is one of the greatest theological questions I have ever been asked. What did I answer? I told him the story of my son and his buddy in the den and then the story of the biologist! And I reminded him of Eric Liddel, the Olympic champion, in the movie Chariots of Fire and that powerful scene when he said to his sister, "God made me fast, and when I run I feel his pleasure."

My golfer friend had also forgotten the good news of Immanuel. The troll had him thinking that God was merely a spectator—up there somewhere watching the game. Thus, he saw his delight in golf as his rather than as the Father's. He saw himself in troll terms with God on one side and himself on the other. Golf was strictly on our side of the table and he wanted to know how he could glorify God in it.

But the truth is that golf is not his domain. It has been invaded by Jesus Christ. It is one of the habitations, the dwelling places, of the Triune life. What do you think? Is Jesus up there in some celestial prison waiting for us to get our religion right? Has he vacated the premises, left us as orphans[26] outside the circle of his family life? Is he no more than a monk who created a religious order? I think not.

Immanuel is not an invitation. It is the truth. Jesus Christ is not

26 See John 14:18.

absent, but present. He is wonderfully and humbly and secretly sharing himself and his life with his Father with us. It is this divine dance, this circle of delight and joy, beauty and excellence and glory, and nothing less, that inhabits our golfer's heart, inspires him and thrills him. Jesus Christ couldn't care less if we glorify him in golf. His passion is that we play golf in his glory.

How does God fit into golf? The real question is, would the game be any fun at all without him? Would living be any fun without him? Well, of course it wouldn't! Living without sharing in this circle of life would be pure drudgery. For what makes relationships, friendships and conversations so good; what makes work, teaching, doctoring and caring so noble; what makes baseball, gardening, fishing, and racing cars so enjoyable; what makes art, music and dancing so alive is that they are all, in their deepest sense, the dwelling places of the Triune life of Father, Son and Spirit.

Immanuel means that human existence has been baptized in the glory, the fullness, the excellence, the beauty, the life of the Triune God. Our problem is not that we have been excluded, any more than the kid was excluded from the fair or the Dwarfs were excluded from Narnia. Our problem is that we believe the troll's whisper, "I am not… ." We live, day in and day out, with our insides so shredded and our security so overwhelmed we suffer from acute Dwarfitis. We cannot see the glory. "It's just golf, just baseball, just fishing. It's just grocery shopping and cooking and cleaning, just supper. It's just botany, just work, just sunshine, just flowers, just music. It's just my daughter coming in to bother me again." The troll has made such mincemeat of our hearts we do not see what is really happening in us and around us. We have no idea what great and astounding thing has been granted to us. We do not know who we really are. We raise golden goblets of rich red wine, but taste only dirty water from a donkey's trough! And then we spend our lives moving from one thing to another in one long, desperate and frantic search for a glass of real wine! But the gospel is really quite simple. Over against the troll's whisper, "I am not…," the Father is shouting His eternal word, "Thou art Mine! and is calling us to answer, "Yes, I am!"

Other Books by C. Baxter Kruger

The Parable of the Dancing God

Building on Jesus' story of a father and his two sons, Dr. Kruger's first—and now internationally best-selling—book is a short and powerful picture of the shocking truth about God. Far from being a bookkeeping legalist, who watches us like a hawk to see if we keep His rules, the Father Jesus reveals is a passionate Father who loves us forever, and desires nothing from us except that we know His acceptance and delight and live in their freedom. Loved around the world and used by pastors, therapists and recovery groups everywhere, this little book brings you face to face with the Father heart of God. It is simple, direct and fearlessly beautiful.

"I had tried for 55 years, 11 months, and 16 days to get it right. I mean, tried really hard. It was after 11 o'clock that night when I decided I had to read this little booklet "Parable of the Dancing God" my son-in-law had sent me. When I got to about the third page, I felt like I had been hit in the face with an iron frying pan. I laid back on the pillow, bewildered, and said, "God, have I been thinking wrong all my life?" The response was a simple and clear, "Yes." And that is just the tip of the iceberg.

Julian Fagan,
Attorney, Amory, Mississippi

The Shack Revisited

Millions have found their spiritual hunger satisfied by William P. Young's #1 *New York Times* bestseller *The Shack* – the story of a man lifted from the depths of despair through his life altering encounter with God the Father, God the Son and God the Holy Spirit. C. Baxter Kruger's *The Shack Revisited* guides readers Into a deeper understanding of these three persons to help readers have a more profound connection with the core message of *The Shack* – that God is love.

"Baxter Kruger will stun readers with his unique cross of intellectual brilliance and creative genius as he takes them deep into the wonder, worship, and possibility that is the world of *The Shack*."

Wm. Paul Young
Author of *The Shack* and *Eve*

Patmos:

Three Days, Two Men
One Extraordinary Conversation

When Aidan finds himself far from his native Mississippi, he inexplicably meets the Apostle John on the isle of Patmos. Beaten down by the modern world and desperate for answers his years of study have failed to satisfy, Aidan is confronted with astounding insight from the beloved disciple of Jesus. The two begin an extraordinary dialogue of truth and lies, revelation and deception, sorrow and joy. Second Edition

Through dreams and mind-bending discussions, the wise apostle exposes the lie of all lies about Jesus, leaving Aidan shaken to the core . . . but liberated. Transformed, Aidan is eager to learn more.

But when John has a vision of the next awakening in Western history, Aidan knows he must return and preach the truth of all truths - before it's too late.

"*Patmos* is a gateway drug to deep and engaging theology and transformation!"

Wm. Paul Young
#1 *New York Times* best-selling author of *The Shack*

Home:

The Inconsolable Dream

Home is among the most evocative and haunting words in our language. Like any other word, it is simply an arrangement of consonants and vowels, yet it possesses the uncanny capacity to speak volumes to us and an almost magical ability to touch our souls. Why is this? What is it about this word? Why does it seem to have such a special ability to touch us so deeply?

For further info on

C. Baxter Kruger

and his books

go to **perichoresis.org**

Ingram Content Group UK Ltd.
Milton Keynes UK
UKHW020912190723
425423UK00001B/154

9 798985 155341